BECO... PROFESSIONAL FOOTBALLER

A Guide on How to be a Good Soccer Midfielder

By

Francis Diaz

TABLE OF CONTENTS

INTRODUCTION

You can pick up motivational playing techniques from a variety of midfield footballers because there are many different types of central midfielders. Due to the wide range of talents needed to master the role, competition among players is fierce. Action-oriented players like Paul Pogba constantly desire the ball and motivate their team. Players like Andres Iniesta continually desire the ball so they can wreak havoc on the opposition with just one touch or pass. N'Golo Kante will steal the ball from the opposition, turning defense into attack in a matter of seconds, and Steven Gerrard will be able to hit a shot from 35 yards out with terrifying accuracy. These are but a few illustrations of the variety of players from whom you might draw inspiration to improve as a central midfielder; there are many more good midfielders.

Despite the variability of the position, every excellent central midfielder should keep these pointers in mind. To assist you to master the role and demonstrate the strength of Pogba and the cutting edge of Iniesta, we've put up a list of advice.

As they are required to play forward and defender roles, the midfielders are a versatile group of players that cover the most territory throughout a match. There are central and wide midfielders, just like there are defenders, as well as players with additional specializations like attacking or defending midfielders. Due to its location between the two penalty areas, the midfield is frequently referred to as the center of the pitch. Here is where soccer will see the most action. Midfielders are the players who start and spend the majority of their time here while alternating between defense and offense, so you can easily spot them.

CHAPTER ONE

TIPS TO HELP YOU MASTER THE ROLE

1.1 ALWAYS BE ON THE MOVE

The most congested part of the field, the middle, can make it challenging to touch the ball in time and space, let alone at all. The best center midfielders are those who are constantly moving, making it difficult for the opposition to mark them, and appearing in spaces that other teams haven't considered covering.

Think about where the ball needs to go and how you might come up with new attacks for your side rather than just concentrating on where it is. The actions you take when you don't have the ball are almost as crucial as those you do when you do.

1.2 PLAY WITH YOUR HEAD UP

Understanding vision is a skill. Certain imaginative and visionary players can see things that others cannot, but there are also various ways you can develop your vision.

The simplest is to play with your head raised. Always keep an eye on the horizon, especially if the ball is not in play. If you see that three of the opposition's defenses are set up on the right, you'll know to alter the play to the opening that has opened up on the left if you win possession. A central midfielder's ability to see spaces and openings is a powerful tool, and it all stems from maintaining a positive attitude.

1.3 MASTER YOUR FIRST TOUCH

Anywhere on the field is necessary for a first touch, but central midfield is considerably more crucial. When you have the football in your possession, you'll have more time to work if you can control it well. A poor first touch can make it easier for the opposition to close you down or may cause you to give up possession entirely, which will put your side under pressure.

1.4 DON'T BE AFRAID TO SHOOT

How frequently do we hear the phrase "guilty of overplaying" concerning football on television? If you obtain a good sight of the goal, don't be scared to fire. Some of the top midfielders in the world are regarded as such due to their importance when it comes to contributing goals; if you don't shoot, you won't score.

1.5 KEEP IT SIMPLE AND STAY COMPOSED

Being a great central midfielder requires a wide variety of passing, yet the most crucial pass you can make is the straightforward one. Even for the top players in the world, 60-yard raking passes and altering the action from one flank to the other present a risk.

Sometimes it's preferable to keep things straightforward. Short, sharp passes make it less likely for you to lose control of the ball because they make the other team work harder to catch it, wearing them out and potentially offering up new opportunities for you. You ought to have success if Pep Guardiola, a legendary coach, did.

1.6 LEARN ABOUT YOUR TEAMMATES

More than any other player, a central midfielder is connected to their team. A center midfielder is a focal point and an important player. It is the posture that ties together left and right as well as defense and offense. As a result, it's crucial to know everything about your colleagues.

You may drop short to pass to and receive from a defender with confidence if you know they are at ease playing the ball out. If your strikers like to play on the last defender's shoulder, you can be sure that they'll be waiting for a through ball at all times. You may become a great center midfielder by building relationships with each player in your squad as well as the other 10 players on the field.

1.7 REPETITION AND SELF-DISCIPLINE

It takes a lot of effort, practice, and attention to one's development to develop into a great center midfielder, but it is possible. Even experienced employees continuously look for ways to enhance their performance because the job is so competitive. The success of their team will be significantly impacted by a quality central midfielder. Finding the time to play match football will be essential to improving as a central midfielder, as the practice is an essential part of any sport's development.

CHAPTER TWO

WHAT YOU MUST DO

2.1 GET SOME EXPERIENCE PLAYING SOCCER

Because the game revolves around you and it takes time to become a good midfielder, central midfield is the most difficult position to master. If you begin playing soccer at a young age, you will have a greater chance of success.

2.2 HAVE GOOD TECHNICAL ABILITY

- Improve your abilities. Because you are the one who holds the ball for the majority of the time and cannot lose the ball, your ball abilities should be above average or excellent.
- You should be skilled at controlling, passing, and receiving the ball with your feet as well as other body parts like your chest and thighs.
- Dribbling is also crucial.

2.3 BE WILLING AND ABLE TO PASS

Avoid playing in the middle if you struggle with passing. The most accomplished athletes disperse the ball play in the midfield. You need to play both in the air and on the ground with quick passes that are properly weighted. You ought to be the player who can read and comprehend the game, identify runs that your teammates are making, and then carry out a pass.

Because they should be able to increase their team's chances of scoring, central midfielders are vital in this regard. They are known as playmakers for a reason.

2.4 WORK ON YOUR DEFENSIVE MANEUVERS

Attacking is just one aspect of central midfield. You are the force behind the team's offensive and defensive operations.

Don't stab too many times. Make the offensive commit a mistake or play the ball backward by forcing them to.

2.5 BE AWARE OF THE BALL AND ANY SHOOTING OPPORTUNITIES.

Always be aware of your surroundings, and when you are off the ball, move toward open space.

2.6 POSSESS SHARP VISION.

You'll be able to move the ball around effectively and generate scoring opportunities as a result. You must direct play as a center midfielder. This entails dispersing the ball and giving each one a once-over.

2.7 WHEN YOU CAN SHOOT.

While the offensive is mostly the responsibility of the strikers, the midfield is not as important, but considering that you are not frequently in the box, a good shot now and then is always a welcome bonus.

CHAPTER THREE

BECOME SUCCESSFUL

You must be proud of your work if you wish to succeed in any position. Players need to approach the game differently and with a variety of talents. Your performance will improve the more you can learn about your profession. You must understand that being a midfielder necessitates being a complete player if you want to be a great midfielder.

You must be skilled at passing, creating plays, and maintaining possession. The ability to read the play, make tackles, and intercept passes are all necessary for midfielders. They must assist in defending and contributing to goals. You are right in the thick of the action as a midfielder. If you are not a complete player, your flaws will be shown.

Don't consider this to be a huge challenge. You take the middle position because you want to participate. You want to influence people. Utilize this as inspiration. To help your team win more games, stand out when you play, and have a great soccer career; work on every aspect of your game.

3.1 HOW TO SUCCEED

Before you can become a competent midfielder in soccer, you must commit to one straightforward mindset:

3.2 DO NOT BE LAZY

It's crucial to work hard in any position on the soccer field. However, compared to other positions, the midfield demands more movement and effort.

The most active position on the soccer pitch is midfield:

Goalkeepers

2-3 miles (3.2-4.8 km) per game

Defenders

4-7 miles (6.4-11.2 km) per game

Midfielders

6-9 miles (9.6 – 14.5 km) per game

Forwards

4-8 to 9.6 kilometers (3.1 to 6 miles) per game

Change your perspective on running and stamina. Anything you fear will inevitably become challenging. You don't need to run. You have the opportunity to accomplish it. That mentality makes you want to run because it sets you apart from your rivals. Work on increasing your endurance so you can perform at your peak in the midfield.

3.3 WHAT A SOCCER MIDFIELDER SHOULD DO

The best technique to improve as a midfielder in soccer is to observe players who currently hold that position in the pros (in this case soccer midfielder). In my experience, the smartest players are typically those who watch the most professional football. They are more aware, have greater vision, and make better decisions.

You can watch professional games or highlights, but you should be aware that viewing is very different from evaluating. You should research the athletes who compete in your position.

Rather than spending the entire time observing the ball. Pay attention to the midfielder you wish to study:

What do they do when they don't have the ball?

What moves do they make to support and assault their teammates?

What choices do they make in particular circumstances?

When do they pass? When do they dribble?

How do they read plays to make tackles or interceptions?

You will get better the more you study and absorb from the top midfielders.

You must train to improve your talents if you hope to become a very excellent midfielder in soccer. However, having a play style that will make you more productive in this particular position is also crucial.

1 – Play forward when possible.

The objective of the game is to score goals. You will always find it difficult to fulfill your position as a playmaker if you are reluctant to play forward passes. Your initial choice should always be to move forward with a teammate you perceive in a forward position. Space to dribble into, take advantage of it without holding back.

2 – Keep possession.

You want to go forward, but doing so in the midfield isn't always an option. You should be very proud of your ability to maintain possession of the ball. Don't cheaply pass the ball in the middle of the field. This could cost your team a lot of money.

3 – Be the outlet.

Always consider how I may help my teammate who owns the ball. Always create passing lanes for your teammates to assist them in escaping difficulty. This holds when goalkeepers, defenders, or even forwards possess the ball. Don't remain still. By giving those options, you can assist your teammates in avoiding difficulties.

3.4 WHAT A MIDFIELDER IN SOCCER SHOULD AVOID DOING

On the other hand, there are some tendencies you should shun if you want to learn how to play soccer as a decent midfielder.

1 – Being careless with your passes.

One errant pass in the middle of the field frequently gives the opposing side chances or even goals. Never lose the ball by making careless or ineffective passes. Our focus tends to wane as we grow weary, not because our talents have declined but rather because our quality has declined. Take pride in every accomplishment.

2 – Getting caught in possession.

When playing as a midfielder in soccer, dribbling in the incorrect places is something to avoid. Attack if there is room to dribble. You occasionally need to use your skills to pull yourself out of a jam. However, it's usually preferable to keep things simple, pass swiftly, and let the ball do the job if there is a lot of pressure or numerous opponents close by.

3 – Slow transition.

All soccer players need to be able to quickly transition from offense to defense, but midfielders especially need to be able to do this. Make the shift from attacking to defending as quickly as possible. Be the first to track back and make a tackle if your team loses the ball. Always keep your head up and be on the lookout for opportunities to score if you win back possession from the opposing side.

It's acceptable to make errors. That is a component of learning. Just be careful not to keep making the same errors. Every setback presents a chance for improvement.

CHAPTER FOUR

QUALITIES OF A GOOD MIDFIELDER

4.1 DEFENSIVE SKILLS

A Defensive midfielder should have excellent defensive abilities, which nearly goes without saying and is stated in the job description. This is likely the most significant role-playing element. If you are capable of doing everything else on this list, but you are unable to defend, you are unlikely to be considered for this position on the squad.

A defensive midfielder serves as the link between the defenders and midfielders while playing at the base of the midfield. By blocking the ball and opposing players from passing them, they are supposed to shield the defenders.

A few characteristics define strong defense. One is being able to regularly tackle well. You must have the ability to quickly insert your foot into the play to stop the ball and avoid fouling the opposing player. And be able to react quickly enough to the ball as it enters the air to get your head on it before the adversary.

To prevent any other players from stealing the ball off you, you must also be able to shield the ball when you have it. The last thing you want to happen is to lose the ball close to your own goal.

4.2. AWARENESS

A defensive midfielder's job requires them to be fully aware of everything that is happening on the field.

Now, this might sound implausible, and, indeed, nobody will ever know with absolute certainty where everyone is and what is happening in their immediate surroundings. However, when you watch a top defensive midfielder in action, it nearly seems as though they possess this talent. When they have the ball, a big part of their job is to be able to start the play as soon as feasible. The quicker they can choose where to play the ball, the quicker their team can transition from a defensive to an offensive posture.

Defensive midfielders must constantly be aware of what is happening around them. If you want to get better at this game, make it a point to pay close attention to everything that is going on around you over the next few games you play. Make it a goal to take in as much of the scene as you can. You will get more natural at doing this as you practice.

4.3. CONDITIONING/STRENGTH AND STAMINA

Defensive midfielder play requires a very high level of physical fitness and endurance. Some of the top midfielders have been calculated to be able to run more than 7 miles (11 km) in a single 90-minute span. This includes "up to 1,300 changes in activity intensity over a 90-minute game," according to a study. This is no easy task!

They must be able to cover the entire field at all times, be alert to where the ball is, and be prepared to thwart any advancing players.

The player needs to adhere to a rigorous fitness regimen to maintain this level of performance over the entire season. This will consist of:

1. Consistent exercise to keep and build up a high degree of stamina.
2. Get enough rest to fully recover from the grueling exercise they continuously subject their bodies to.
3. Ensure that they consume the right foods each day to power their bodies properly.
4. Hydration to replenish every drop of fluid lost. All of these things will help them get to their physical peak, which will enable them to perform at their very best.

4.4. DISCIPLINE/POSITIONING

Having discipline is essential when playing this role for a soccer team. You will be relied upon by the team. This is true for the entire squad, not just the defensive midfielder, but it's crucial for them in particular. This midfielder is surrounded by certain teams.

Every one of their plays is intended to pass through this player. And much as in reality, if a crucial component is absent, the entire system may malfunction.

These players won't be in the appropriate spot when they are needed if they lack a high level of discipline when it comes to maintaining their position. They must be able to resist the urge to leave their position when it is not required.

4.5. EXCELLENT VISION AND PASSING RANGE

The defensive midfielder frequently serves as the team's playmaker as well. They are in charge of managing the game's flow. As necessary, move the ball from front to rear or from side to side. They must be able to pass the ball precisely where they want it to go to move the ball around effectively and efficiently. It is insufficient to simply kick the ball in one direction and hope for the best. They also need to have a keen vision to determine where the ball should go. Where the ball needs to go must be visible to them.

A defensive midfielder can make the difference between their team winning or losing a soccer match if they can look up, anticipate where one of their attacking players will be before they arrive, and pass the ball precisely to that location.

4.6. ABILITY TO READ THE GAME

When a player can read a game, it means they have a phenomenal capacity for foresight and comprehension, oftentimes even before events have taken place. They appear to have the ability to foresee where a player will pass the ball before they even pass it, or where an opponent will be on the pitch and can move to that location before the opponent does.

The defensive midfielder will play their part in the game better and contribute to the success of their side if they are adept at reading the game.

4.7. TACKLE WELL

This was stated in passing above, but it deserves to be highlighted separately as well. The effectiveness of a tackle can determine whether the opponent is allowed to advance to the goal.

Timing is everything while tackling another player. Going in too soon can cause the opposing player to spot you coming and possibly alter their course so they can go right past you. Go in too late, and you can wind up taking out the opposing player and awarding a deadly free kick. It takes time and practice to become a good tackler. The difference between competent and outstanding defensive midfielders can often be found in their ability to time a tackle effectively and execute it.

The slide tackle is the kind of tackle that demands the most precise timing while also having the most spectacular visual impact. A player can rescue their team from difficulty and look good doing it if they can complete a slide tackle. You need to be confident that your shin guards will adequately protect you if you want to tackle with confidence. I suggest taking a look at these shin guards on Amazon. They are made to provide convenience and safety simultaneously.

4.8. COMMUNICATE WELL

Each player will be able to play much better as a member of the team with effective communication on the field of play during a game. Any effective team must be able to communicate effectively with one another. They must comprehend what each of them are contemplating, their course of action, and their plans. Without it, each player might be working alone, unaware of what the other players on the field are trying to accomplish. And this can only result in misunderstanding, which can never result in efficient teamwork but simply a mess and a dysfunctional group.

Due to their position at the heart of the squad, defensive midfielders have an edge in the communication department. Any other player on the field can shout at them from a short distance away. They are the only ones who can communicate with the other members of the team. Any excellent defensive midfielder will spend time outside of games honing their communication skills with the rest of their squad because of this position and job.

4.9. STAY CALM

A defensive midfielder must be able to maintain composure while the ball is coming their way and they must decide what to do in a split second.

You're going to make all kinds of mistakes if you're panicking right now or having trouble thinking clearly. The player must be able to assess the scenario with objectivity and occasionally make decisions on the fly.

Now, keep in mind that being relaxed is not the same as being tranquil. The midfielder won't be prepared to respond when necessary if they are simply comfortable. They might not be paying attention, in which case the game and the opposing players might pass them by before they even realize it.

The athlete will be able to perform at their peak without being adversely affected by everything that is happening around them if they can maintain their composure in any situation that is fraught with stress.

4.10. MAINTAIN A HIGH LEVEL OF CONCENTRATION

It can be difficult to maintain your focus on the game you are playing for 90 minutes, or even longer unless you have adequately trained for it. In a soccer match, the outcome might change at any time; therefore the players must be prepared to react right away.

When a player is not actively participating in the action, they should not allow their thoughts to wander. Otherwise, they risk being caught off guard when the ball suddenly comes their way and falling behind the other players in figuring out what to do. Due to the position they fill, defensive midfielders must constantly be focused on what is happening in the game around them. Even if the ball is in a different area of the field, kids still need to be paying attention and taking in the action. The player's ability to make quick decisions when they are called upon to act will be significantly improved by maintaining focus at all times.

4.11. ABILITY TO BREAK UP PLAY

Another simple but crucial component of a defensive midfielder's job description is the capacity to effectively stop play throughout a match. The ability to step in and intercept the ball or otherwise interfere with the other team's momentum when they are heading toward your goal and appear to be about to launch an attack on it can be the difference between winning and losing a game. A great defensive midfielder will be capable of doing this repeatedly.

A high-caliber defensive midfielder can annoy the opposition if they consistently believe that every time they advance with the ball, their attack fails. And this may result in even more errors from the opposing squad. A player who excels at breaking up plays might infuse his or her squad with an increasing amount of confidence. And as a result, the team will be more confident in their collective ability and have a better chance of winning the game.

4.12. TACTICAL AWARENESS

A defensive midfielder in a soccer match needs to be strategically alert at all times. They need to understand what is expected of the team in terms of tactics because they frequently possess the ball, move it across the field, and initiate attacks.

Understanding your team's playing arrangement and the positions of the other members of your squad is crucial. Before a game, the coach will frequently spend time with the defensive midfielder outlining the team's goals for the contest. The defensive midfielder will then make sure that their choices during the game are in line with the team's coaching philosophy. They must also be aware of what is going on in the game to successfully adjust to its constantly shifting flow. How effectively the game's tactics are executed will frequently be determined by the defensive midfielder.

4.13. EFFECTIVELY SHIELD THE DEFENDERS

The defensive midfielder's function as a defense shield is one aspect of their job that we haven't yet covered. To be closer to the defense, the defensive midfielder may frequently stand a little farther back than the rest of the team. As the first line of defense, they take over. The goal is to reach the ball quickly and prevent it from reaching your team's defenders. Defensive midfielders will do this by moving over the field's width to position themselves where they are needed as the ball is brought down the field toward them. They will use every effort to get the ball before any of the defenders behind them can.

4.14. CONFIDENCE IN ABILITIES

It's also important for a defensive midfielder to have self-assurance. To be the best they can be when they go out to play the game, they need to have dedicated all the hours they have to practice, train and become ready. They will have the assurance that they are performing to their highest potential at that precise moment because of the preparation they did in advance.

Being self-assured offers defensive midfielders the assurance that they can carry out their duties, which is why it is so crucial to this aspect of their job. If you've ever been around someone who lacks self-assurance, you've probably noticed that they don't do a very good job of announcing their presence. A superb defensive midfielder needs to make their presence known to everyone nearby. They must control the field of play and make their presence felt the entire time.

4.15. SPEED

A big benefit is having quick players.

1. The field will be easier for you to navigate.
2. You will be able to move with the ball more quickly.
3. You'll also be able to bounce back from errors more quickly.

It is important to put as much effort as possible into developing your speed when preparing for a soccer match.

This is similar to playing any other position for a defensive midfielder. A defensive midfielder's capacity to be more effective in their position increases with speed.

While some of the best defensive midfielders were not particularly quick, it must be acknowledged that some of them were. They were in the right position at the right time and had the amazing ability to read the game properly, which allowed them to play their roles so expertly. But I'm confident that they would all agree that they could have all been even more useful to the squad if they had been able to combine their skills with even more speed.

4.16. EFFECTIVE LEADERSHIP

Leading your team well during a soccer match helps motivate them to succeed. The other players naturally look to the defensive midfielder to guide them because of the significant orchestrating role a defensive midfielder plays in the team's style of play. The entire squad may suffer if the midfielder is unable to handle the pressure of such a heavy load or does not fulfill this function effectively.

When we discuss leadership, we don't just mean telling the other players what they should do (although this can be an important part of leading). We also discuss setting an example for others. As we just discussed, the defensive midfielder will naturally be looked upon by the other players for leadership. The other players will be motivated to exert equal effort if they witness one player giving the game their all, working tirelessly, and continuing to play their best even when everything appears hopeless.

4.17. WILLING TO SACRIFICE

This role requires you to be willing to compromise on what might make you look better to improve team performance. Nobody enjoys seeing a self-centered player. Everyone is irritated by how ugly it is. The defensive midfielder position in soccer frequently lacks the recognition or glory that some of the other positions do.

The defensive midfielder will likely find themselves out of position at precisely the time when their team needs them to be in that position if they decide they no longer enjoys this and seek out more attention and glory. Due to their unwillingness to comply with team demands, this may result in a lack of team cohesion and the player being dismissed from the squad. Defensive midfielders need to keep in mind that they are playing as a member of a team, and if the team performs well, they will also perform well, even though it can be difficult at times to make the sacrifice.

Printed in Great Britain
by Amazon

34007638R10030